DATE DUE 8/05

DEC 1 9 2005		
JAN 0 9 2006		

DEMCO 38-296

OPRAH WINFREY

KATHERINE KROHN

In Consultation with Martha Cosgrove,
M.A. and Reading Specialist

LERNER PUBLICATIONS COMPANY/MINNEAPOLIS

Martha Cosgrove has a master's degree from the University of Minnesota in secondary education, with an emphasis on developmental and remedial reading. She is licensed in 7–12 English and language arts, developmental reading, and remedial reading. She has had several works published, and she gives numerous state and national presentations in her areas of expertise.

Lerner Publications Company
A division of Lerner Publishing Group
241 First Avenue North
Minneapolis, MN 55401

Website address: www.lernerbooks.com

Library of Congress Cataloging-in-Publication Data

Krohn, Katherine E.
  Oprah Winfrey / by Katherine Krohn.
      p.   cm. – (Just the facts biographies)
  Includes bibliographical references and index.
  ISBN: 0-8225-2472-4 (lib. bdg. : alk. paper)
    1. Winfrey, Oprah—Juvenile literature. 2. Television personalities—United States—Biography—Juvenile literature. 3. Women television personalities—United States—Biography—Juvenile literature. 4. Actors—United States—Biography—Juvenile literature. I. Title. II. Series.
  PN1992.4.W56K76 2005
  791.4502'8'092–dc22   2004005481

Manufactured in the United States of America
1 2 3 4 5 6 – JR – 10 09 08 07 06 05

CONTENTS

CHAPTER 1

FARM GIRL

(Above) Oprah spent her early years on a farm in rural Mississippi.

FOUR-YEAR-OLD Oprah Winfrey stood on the screened-in porch of her grandmother's small farm. She watched her grandmother, Hattie Mae Lee, stir a big black pot of boiling clothes. It was 1958, and Oprah and her grandmother lived in the countryside of Mississippi. Hattie Mae couldn't afford an electric washing machine. Instead, she cleaned her family's dirty clothes in boiling water.

"I remember thinking, my life won't be like this," Oprah said later. "It will be better."

Oprah Gail Winfrey was born on January 29, 1954, in Kosciusko, a small town in central Mississippi. She was born in her grandmother's house with the help of a midwife. A midwife is a woman who delivers babies. Oprah's mother, Vernita Lee, was eighteen and unmarried. She was not in a serious relationship with Oprah's father, Vernon Winfrey. He was a twenty-five-year-old U.S. Army private stationed at Fort Rucker, Alabama.

Vernita wasn't sure what to name the new baby at first. A week after the birth, Vernita's sister, Ida, had an idea. She suggested that Vernita name the new member of the family Orpah, after a character in the Bible. But the name was spelled "Oprah" on the baby's birth certificate by mistake. And her name has been Oprah ever since.

During the 1950s, many African Americans in the small towns of the South were very poor. Many black southerners, tired of being poor, moved to northern states in search of work. It was easier to

IT'S A FACT!

Vernita's new baby girl was the great-great-granddaughter of Constantine and Violet Winfrey. They were Mississippi slaves who had been freed after the Civil War (1861–1865).

find a job in northern cities like Detroit, Michigan; Cleveland, Ohio; Milwaukee, Wisconsin; and New York, New York, than it was in the South.

Oprah was only four years old when her mother decided to pack her bags and move to Milwaukee, Wisconsin—without Oprah. Vernita hoped to find work as a maid and make a better life for herself. She planned to send for her daughter once she found a job.

Vernita left Oprah with Hattie Mae, Oprah's grandmother. Oprah called her grandmother Mama. Mama was very strict, but she also cared deeply for Oprah.

CHORES AND CHURCH

Hattie Mae lived on the edge of Kosciusko, and there were no other children nearby. Oprah wished she had someone to play with. So she made friends with the animals on the farm. She gave names to the chickens and pigs and told them stories.

From an early age, Oprah was expected to do chores around the farm. Her grandmother taught her to hang the laundry on the clothesline with wooden clothespins. She also showed Oprah how to make soap from lye, a strong-smelling, powdery white chemical.

RACE IN THE 1950s

When Oprah was a child, it was common for people to be judged by the color of their skin. This racial prejudice was especially common in southern states. For decades, many public schools in the United States were segregated. That meant black kids went to all-black schools and white kids went to all-white schools. In 1954, the year Oprah was born, the U.S. Supreme Court (the highest court in the nation) made a decision. Racial segregation would no longer be allowed in public schools.

Still, other public places in the South remained segregated. Black people were not allowed to use anything marked "whites only," such as drinking fountains and restrooms. Hotels, churches, theaters, and restaurants were segregated. On buses, black riders had to sit in a separate section at the back of the bus. They had to give up their seat if a white person wanted to sit there.

In December 1955, something happened in Montgomery, Alabama, that led to change. An African American woman named Rosa Parks was riding a bus. A white man wanted to sit in her row. Parks refused to give up her seat and was arrested. Her brave action led other African Americans to protest her arrest and the bus segregation laws. Black people in Montgomery refused to ride the buses for 382 days. The bus company lost a lot of money. Because of the protests, the bus company changed its rules so the buses were no longer segregated.

The story of the success of this protest inspired people across the country. They began fighting against segregated businesses in other communities. They fought so that all Americans could enjoy their civil rights (personal freedoms). The fight became known as the civil rights movement.

Some of Oprah's tasks were harder than others. Hattie Mae showed her how to kill hogs and chickens. She killed the chickens by wringing, or twisting, their thin necks. "Watch me, 'cause you're going to have to learn how to do this," said Hattie Mae. But Oprah had different plans for her future. "Don't need to watch Grandma," she thought, "because my life isn't going to be like this."[3]

Hattie Mae's house did not have indoor plumbing. Oprah's main chore was to carry water from the well every morning and night. Oprah and her grandmother used the water for drinking, washing dishes, and cleaning themselves with a washcloth. On Saturday nights, Oprah took her weekly tub bath, using water heated on the stove. The next day, she and Mama would be fresh and clean for church.

Oprah's family couldn't afford toys from a store. She had a favorite doll that her grandmother made from a corncob. Although the doll was plain, Oprah thought she was beautiful.

Hattie Mae wanted Oprah to grow up reading the Bible. So she had taught Oprah to read when she was only three years old. She encouraged Oprah to memorize passages from the Bible and other religious books. Young Oprah had a very good memory. She quickly memorized her Bible verses.

Hattie Mae was proud of her granddaughter and wanted to show her off. She arranged for Oprah to speak at church services at Kosciusko Baptist Church. On Easter Sunday, Oprah stood up to speak in public for the first time. She smiled and spoke confidently in her high-pitched, little-girl voice. "Jesus rose on Easter Day, Hallelujah, Hallelujah . . . all the angels did proclaim."

IT'S A FACT!

Kosciusko, Mississippi, is named after a Polish patriot, Tadeusz Kosciuszko. He had helped the American colonists during the American Revolution (1775–1783).

Hattie Mae smiled proudly from her seat in the front row. A woman sitting nearby leaned toward her. "[Hattie Mae], this child is gifted," she whispered, fanning herself with a paper fan.

Oprah's grandmother nodded as the church people praised Oprah's speaking ability. Everyone was impressed that a small child could speak so smoothly and clearly.

Oprah had other chances to recite, or speak from memory, when Hattie Mae had company over to the house. "I would just get up in front of her friends and start doing pieces I had memorized," Oprah said. "Everywhere I went, I'd say, 'Do you want to hear me do something?'"

Oprah was encouraged to recite Bible passages. But most other times, she was discouraged from talking in public. Hattie Mae, like many people in her generation, expected children to be "seen and not heard." Children were supposed to stay quiet except when spoken to by an adult.

Oprah's grandmother also believed in the Bible phrase, "Spare the rod and spoil the child." In other words, she felt that children should be punished by being hit. Otherwise, they were likely to grow up spoiled and disrespectful. Oprah was lively and full of spirit. She was beaten almost daily.

Oprah's heart sank whenever her grandmother told her to "go get a switch." That meant Oprah was in for another "switching," or beating with a stick. She had to cut a tree branch herself and bring it to her grandmother.

SCHOOL DAYS

In the fall of 1959, Oprah started kindergarten in the nearby town of Buffalo, Mississippi. Unlike the other children in her class, five-year-old Oprah could already read and write. She quickly became bored with the simple play and basic lessons of kindergarten.

One day soon after school began, Oprah wrote a note to her teacher, Miss Knew. She wasn't sure how to spell her teacher's name, but she did her best. Oprah's teacher read the carefully printed words: "DEAR MISS NEW. I DO NOT THINK I BELONG HERE."

The teacher was very surprised that Oprah could already write. Right away, she had Oprah moved into the first-grade class.

Soon Oprah faced a different kind of move. By 1960, her grandmother had become ill. Oprah was sent to live with her mother in Milwaukee. She left Mississippi, and her grandmother, forever.

CHAPTER 2
WHERE IS MY HOME?

OPRAH'S MOTHER grabbed Oprah's book out of her hand. Six-year-old Oprah felt her pulse race and her face get hot. "You're nothing but a bookworm!" her mother yelled. "You think you're better than other kids! Get your butt outside!" Oprah fought back tears and went outside. What was wrong with loving books? she wondered.

Vernita Lee, Oprah's mother, had little education. She didn't understand the beauty and power of books. She discouraged her daughter from reading. And she refused to take Oprah to the public library, the place Oprah most wanted to go.

Oprah didn't like her new home in Milwaukee. It was an industrial city—it had many businesses and factories. It was noisy and crowded with people. Everything seemed so strange and different from life on the farm in Kosciusko. Oprah missed her grandmother, her teacher and schoolmates, and people at church.

Vernita lived in a single room in a boardinghouse on Ninth Street. A boardinghouse is a house where rooms are rented and meals are included in the rent. Vernita worked as a maid, cleaning the homes of white people. Her pay was lower than she had hoped to earn. And Vernita had two children to feed. She had recently given birth to her second child, Patricia. Oprah now had a baby half-sister.

Vernita worked long, difficult hours. Still, she sometimes had to rely on welfare to make ends meet. (Welfare is money provided by the U.S. government to low-income families.) She had little time to care for Oprah and the new baby. When Vernita did have time at home, she showered the baby with affection, ignoring Oprah.

"[Patricia] was adored because she was light-skinned," Oprah said later. "My half-sister and mother slept inside. I was put out on the porch."

UPROOTED AGAIN

The demands of working at her job and raising two children were too much for Oprah's mother. She often left Oprah and Patricia with neighbors in the boardinghouse or with a cousin who lived nearby. Oprah lived with her mother for a little more than a year. In early 1962, Vernita decided that Oprah should go stay with her father in Nashville, Tennessee, for a while. In the meantime, Vernita figured, she would look for a better home for her daughters.

Oprah didn't know her father, Vernon Winfrey, very well. She hadn't seen him since she was a small child. And she had never been to Tennessee. She wasn't sure what to expect.

Oprah had never been to Nashville, Tennessee. She went there to live with her father in 1962.

Vernon had moved to Nashville after his service in the U.S. Army. Nashville was a big, successful city known as the home of the country music industry. Vernon had married a woman named Zelma. He had also bought a one-story brick house with white shutters. He worked two jobs as a janitor. One was at a hospital and the other was at Vanderbilt University in Nashville.

Vernon and Zelma were very happy to have seven-year-old Oprah join their household. They loved kids and were unable to have children of their own. Oprah felt welcome in their home right away. She was thrilled to discover that, for the first time in her life, she would have her own bedroom and bed.

In school, Oprah was ahead of most children her age. So she skipped a grade in her new school, Wharton Elementary School, in Nashville. Instead of being in second grade, Oprah would be in third. Her father and stepmother wanted Oprah to be prepared for third grade. They spent many hours helping her learn what she needed to strengthen her language and math skills.

Vernon and Zelma were strict parents. They believed that children needed structure in their lives. Vernon and Zelma were not educated themselves, but they understood the importance of schoolwork and reading.

A READER AND SPEAKER

Oprah's father and stepmother took her to the library soon after she arrived in Nashville. To Oprah's delight, they insisted that she get a library card. "Getting my library card was like citizenship, it was like American citizenship," remembered Oprah.

Oprah liked to daydream. Sometimes she imagined herself as a character in the book she was reading. "I read a book in the third grade about Katie John, who hated boys, and she had freckles," said Oprah. "Well, Lord knows, I'm not going to have freckles, no way, no how. But I tried to put some on. And I went through 'my Katie John phase.'"

IT'S A FACT

Katie John Tucker is the creation of Mary Calhoun. First published in the 1960s, the Katie John series has a loyal following among girl readers. Katie John is a warm-hearted, impulsive tomboy. She gets into many scrapes but still comes out feeling positive and in charge of her life.

Vernon and Zelma required Oprah to write book reports on the books she checked out of the library. She also had to complete her regular school assignments. Oprah didn't mind the extra work. She liked to read and study. And she liked the fact that her father and stepmother paid so much attention to her.

Vernon and Zelma were active members of Faith Missionary Baptist Church in Nashville. They were pleased to see how well Oprah could recite Bible passages and stories. Oprah began speaking in church, as she had in Kosciusko.

Once she recited a sermon, or religious speech, called "Invictus" by William Ernest Henley. "At the time I was saying it, I didn't know what I was talking about," Oprah recalled. "But I'd do all the motions, 'O-U-T OF THE NIGHT THAT covers me,' and people would say, 'Whew, that child can speak.'"

Vernon and Zelma took Oprah to speak at churches all over Nashville. She became known as the Speaker—the young girl who could speak so well. With her talents encouraged and blossoming in Nashville, Oprah felt truly happy for the first time in a long time.

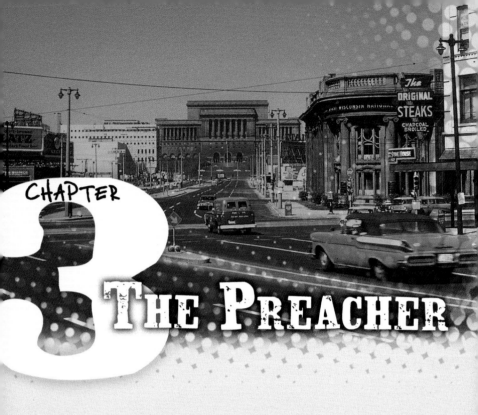

CHAPTER 3

THE PREACHER

WHEN THE SCHOOL YEAR ended in 1962, eight-year-old Oprah traveled back to Milwaukee. It was time for a summer visit with her mother. When Oprah saw her mother again, she was surprised. So much had changed in the past year.

(Above) Oprah moved back to Milwaukee in late 1962.

Vernita had moved to a two-bedroom apartment with Patricia. And she had another baby, a boy named Jeffrey. In Milwaukee, Oprah shared a bedroom with her half-brother and half-sister. She spent the summer reading and looking after Patricia and Jeffrey. She didn't see much of her mother, who worked long hours. When Vernita was home, she spent most of her time caring for her youngest children.

As autumn approached, Vernon arrived in Milwaukee to take Oprah back to Nashville. But Oprah told him she wanted to stay in Milwaukee. She missed her father, her stepmother, and her house in Nashville. But she wanted to please her mother. Disappointed, Vernon returned by himself to Nashville.

Oprah busied herself with schoolwork. She liked the fourth grade. She especially admired her teacher, Mrs. Mary Duncan. Mrs. Duncan treated Oprah like she was a special person. She gave Oprah the attention, advice, and direction she wasn't getting from her mother.

When Oprah was young, many public schools set aside time during the day for "devotion." This included Bible readings, religious lessons, and prayer. Mrs. Duncan often asked Oprah to lead the daily devotion in class. Some of Oprah's classmates didn't like her, because she was smart and good at reciting. They called her Preacher Woman.

Each Sunday in church, Oprah would memorize the minister's sermon, or speech. Then she recited bits and pieces of the sermon during devotion periods the next week. "My, my, that's just lovely, Miss Oprah Gail," Mrs. Duncan said.

LONELY GIRL

At home, Oprah didn't get nearly as much attention. She often turned to television for company. TV was still rather new in the early 1960s. Most U.S. households were just getting television sets.

Oprah's favorite TV shows were about happy families. She loved *Leave It to Beaver,* a funny show about a boy named Beaver Cleaver and his family. She also enjoyed the popular show *I Love Lucy,* featuring comedian Lucille Ball. Oprah thought she might want to be an actress someday. She might be a famous star like the ones she saw on television and in movies.

Actress Lucille Ball in a scene from *I Love Lucy*

Oprah continued to recite sermons and stories in church. She loved to speak–for anyone who would listen. "From the time I was eight years old, I was a champion speaker," she said. "I spoke for every women's group, banquet, church function."

Oprah loved the attention and praise she received when she spoke in public. But privately, she was a lonely child. She deeply wanted love and affection from her mother. But Vernita was usually too busy to give Oprah the care and attention she wanted.

Vernita often left Oprah and her half-brother and half-sister with a babysitter. One evening in 1963, when Oprah was nine years old, her mother went out. Vernita left the children in the care of their nineteen-year-old male cousin. That night, Oprah's cousin raped her. Afterward, she was trembling and shaking and crying. Her cousin took her out for an ice cream cone. He told her not to tell anyone what he had done.

A couple of years after that attack, Oprah was sexually abused by a family friend and then by an uncle. For several years, Oprah was sexually abused often. "It was just an ongoing, continuous thing," she

IT'S A FACT!

Oprah had few places to go to get help against child abuse. That's not true anymore. The counselors at Childhelp USA® are available every day. They can be contacted for free by phone at 1-800-422-4453. Their website is <http://childhelpusa.org>. It has a special section for kids and teens.

said. "So much so, that I started to think, you know, 'This is the way life is.'"

When Oprah was a child, most people did not know much about childhood sexual abuse. It was not talked about openly, and no laws existed to protect children. Oprah figured that no one would believe her if she told the truth. She thought she would be blamed for being sexually abused. So, feeling confused and helpless, she kept silent. She tried not to think about the abuse. She concentrated on her schoolwork, on reciting in church, and on reading books for fun.

In books, Oprah could lose herself in other worlds and forget her troubles for a while. When she was a young teenager, Oprah's favorite book was Betty Smith's *A Tree Grows in Brooklyn*. It is the story of Francie Nolan, a lonely but hopeful poor girl growing up in Brooklyn, New York, in the early 1900s.

Oprah stayed up all night long reading the book in the small bedroom that she shared with Patricia and Jeffrey. "There was a tree outside my apartment, and I used to imagine it was the same tree," remembered Oprah. "I felt like my life was like [Francie Nolan's]."

In spite of her difficulties at home, Oprah did well in school and earned good grades. But she spent a lot of time alone and had few friends.

UPWARD BOUND

In the mid-1960s, Oprah started attending Lincoln Middle School in downtown Milwaukee. One of the teachers at Lincoln was a man named Gene Abrams. He saw Oprah reading in the school cafeteria every day. Oprah was different from the other students. She wasn't rowdy and loud. She wasn't surrounded by chatty friends like the other girls. Instead, she was quiet and liked to study. She was always reading a book.

Abrams decided to help Oprah. He helped her transfer to Nicolet High School. Nicolet was an all-white school in the Milwaukee suburb of Glendale.

There, Oprah could take part in a program called Upward Bound. Oprah had earned good grades. Through the program, she would have a chance for a better education.

Oprah was both excited and nervous about changing schools. Her daily routine changed a lot. She had to ride three buses to get to the suburban school. She was the only African American student there. Oprah still spoke with a southern accent, so she didn't talk like the other kids, either. Most of the students at Nicolet were nice to Oprah, and she quickly made friends. But she wasn't sure if people liked her because of who she was or because she was black. "In 1968 it was real hip to know a black person, so I was very popular," Oprah recalled.

It was easy to see the difference between her life and the lives of her white friends. She felt

IT'S A FACT

A law, called the Economic Opportunities Act, created Upward Bound in 1964. The program helps bright students from low-income families. The goal is for the students to do well in college entrance tests so they can get into colleges and universities.

Oprah was the only African American at Nicolet High School.

poor. She wished she had nice clothes and a big house like the kids at Nicolet High.

Oprah liked her friends, but she couldn't really relate to them. The students at Nicolet had not known many black people–and it showed. "The kids would all bring me back to their houses, . . . bring out their maid from the back and say, 'Oprah, do you know Mabel?'" Oprah remembered.

TROUBLED TEEN

Life at home was also difficult. Oprah still wished for more affection from her mother. Vernita seemed to like Patricia and Jeffrey more than her. Meanwhile, she was still being sexually abused. She had no one to talk to about her experience and feelings. Her unhappiness showed in her behavior. She became wilder during her teen years.

In 1968, when Oprah was fourteen, she was having trouble reading. Her mother took her to an eye doctor. The doctor told Oprah that she needed glasses. Oprah's mother chose the least expensive frames for the eyeglasses. They were old-fashioned frames and shaped like butterflies. Oprah wanted a pair of stylish, attractive glasses. Vernita told her they couldn't afford nicer frames. But Oprah wasn't ready to give up.

She waited until her mother left for work one day. Then Oprah stomped on the new glasses, crushing them to bits. She wanted to make the living room look like someone had broken in. So she knocked a lamp to the floor and tore down the curtains. Next she called the police. "We've been robbed," she cried.

When the police arrived at the apartment, Oprah was laid out on the floor. She pretended someone had hit her on the head and knocked her out. The officer was suspicious. He thought Oprah might be faking the robbery.

But when Oprah "came to," the officer took her to the hospital. Workers there called Oprah's mother. Vernita rushed to the hospital in a panic. She, too, wondered if Oprah was acting, but she wasn't sure. In the end, Oprah's trick worked. Her mother bought her a new pair of glasses.

Oprah's behavior grew wilder and wilder. She skipped school, dated many boys, and stole money from her mother's purse. She ran away from home more than once.

One time when Oprah ran away, she headed for downtown Milwaukee. There she saw a big limousine in front of a fancy hotel. Oprah spotted Aretha Franklin, the famous singer, stepping out of the limo. Oprah quickly made a plan. She boldly ran up to Aretha and told her

Aretha Franklin

a wild story. She said her parents had kicked her out of the house and she needed to buy a bus ticket to go stay with relatives in Ohio. Reportedly, Aretha felt sorry for Oprah. She handed her a crisp one-hundred-dollar bill. Oprah happily took the money and stayed in a hotel for a few days. In the hotel room, she lived it up, watching TV and ordering room service.

Oprah's mother didn't understand what had happened to her daughter. Just a few years earlier, Oprah had been a sweet, quiet girl. Vernita could see that something was wrong, but she didn't know what to do to help. Eventually, her patience wore thin. She looked for another home for Oprah. She called a detention home for troubled teens. But the institution was full. Vernita decided to send Oprah back to her father's house in Nashville.

Oprah didn't know if her father would want her either. But she was heading to Nashville anyway.

CHAPTER 1

PRIZE WINNER

OPRAH'S FATHER and stepmother were happy to have her back. They had missed her, and they welcomed her back into their cozy house in Nashville.

But Vernon and Zelma didn't approve of Oprah's grown-up new look. She wore short miniskirts and heavy makeup. She also had a sassy new attitude. Vernon felt that Oprah's mother hadn't provided her with proper care and direction. He wanted to get Oprah "back on track" in Nashville.

Even with the rules, Oprah was glad to be back in her father's home. Vernon and Zelma's house seemed like a mansion compared to her mother's small apartment. They weren't wealthy, but they had plenty of food and money to buy clothes for Oprah. Vernon now owned his own barbershop.

Vernon did not know that Oprah had been

sexually abused in Milwaukee. Oprah hid another secret from him, too. She was pregnant. She was afraid and ashamed to tell him the truth. She hid her pregnancy, wearing baggy clothing until her seventh month. At that point, Oprah's belly was very round. She knew she had to tell her father. On the day she broke the news, she was even more upset than her father was. She was so stressed, in fact, that she went into early labor. She gave birth to the baby that day. The tiny infant died within two weeks.

After her baby died, Oprah felt a mixture of sadness and relief. At age fourteen, she didn't feel ready to be a parent. Oprah never said who the baby's father was.

A FRESH START

In September 1968, Oprah began tenth grade at East High School in Nashville. Because she'd skipped

second grade, Oprah was younger than the other tenth-graders. She was still adjusting to losing her baby and moving to a new school. At first, her grades were almost all Cs. Vernon pushed Oprah to try harder.

"If you were a child who could only get Cs, then that is all I would expect of you," he told her. "But you are not. So, in this house, Cs are not acceptable."

Oprah tried to see the loss of her baby as a lesson. In a way, she had been given a second chance in life. She was determined to turn her grades, and her life, around.

Throughout high school, Oprah continued to read a great deal. She especially liked books about women who showed courage in getting through hard times. She read about Anne Frank, the Jewish girl who had kept a diary while her family hid from Hitler's Nazis during World War II (1939–1945). She read about Helen Keller, who lived a full, rich life even though she was blind, deaf, and couldn't talk. Oprah also admired Sojourner Truth. Truth fought for the end of slavery. She also fought for women's rights long before the women's suffrage (right to vote) movement of the early 1900s.

When Oprah was sixteen, she read an autobiography that affected her deeply. It was Maya Angelou's 1970 best-seller, *I Know Why the Caged Bird Sings*. Like Oprah, Angelou was raised in the South by her grandmother. She later lived with her mother and then her father. She was raped as a child and found comfort in books.

"I read it over and over," said Oprah. "I had never before read a book

IT'S A FACT!

Little did Oprah know that Maya Angelou would later become one of her closest friends. Oprah gave Angelou a huge sixty-fifth birthday celebration in 1993. That same year, Angelou dedicated a book of poetry to Oprah.

that validated my own existence [described similar
life situations]."

Vernon and Zelma Winfrey continued to
encourage Oprah's studies as well as her talent for
public speaking. "We knew she had great potential.
We knew she had a gift and talent to act and
speak," said Oprah's father. "She's never been a
backseat person, in school or in church. She always
loved the limelight."

Oprah attended Faith Missionary Baptist
Church each Sunday with her father and stepmother.
She sometimes gave Bible readings there. She also
spoke at other area churches and clubs.

Her talent earned her wider recognition in
1970. That year, she won a speech contest
sponsored by the Elks Club. Oprah was filled with
happiness when she took the prize, a four-year
college scholarship. A scholarship is money for
school, awarded for doing something well. She
would begin looking at her college options next
year, when she was a senior.

WINNING CONTESTS

Besides earning good grades in school, Oprah was
also popular. In 1971, Oprah ran for vice president

of the student council. Her slogan was "Vote for the Grand Ole Oprah." It was a funny takeoff on the Grand Ole Opry, the famous Nashville concert hall for country music. Oprah was thrilled when she won the election.

Later that year, Oprah and another student were chosen to represent the state of Tennessee at the White House Conference on Youth. They were chosen because of their excellent grades and leadership abilities. The conference was held in Estes Park, Colorado. Oprah met teens from all over the country. When she returned to Nashville, Oprah was interviewed by disc jockey John Heidelberg on WVOL, a local radio station. He talked to her about her experiences at the conference.

IT'S A FACT

Oprah was often called by her middle name, Gail, throughout high school.

A few months later, Heidelberg called Oprah again. He asked her if she'd like to represent the radio station in the Miss Fire Prevention contest. This was a teen beauty pageant, or contest, in Nashville. Oprah wasn't sure at first. A beauty pageant? She had never thought of herself as a "beauty." But she figured it would be fun to enter anyway.

At the pageant, Oprah paraded before the judges in her new evening gown. She didn't think she stood a chance of winning. No black person had ever won the title of Miss Fire Prevention. And all of Oprah's opponents were white girls with "fire"-red hair. Because she didn't think she had a chance of taking the crown, Oprah felt relaxed and confident.

One part of the contest was a question-and-answer category. The judges asked each contestant a question. The teen was supposed to come up with a thoughtful, intelligent answer. The first question was, "What would you do if you had a million dollars?"

One contestant said she would buy a truck for her father. Another teen proudly said that she would buy her brother a motorcycle and her mother a new Frigidaire refrigerator.

Soon it was Oprah's turn to answer the question. She thought a moment. She decided to just have fun with her answer. "If I had a million dollars," Oprah began, "I would be a spendin' fool. I'm not quite sure what I would spend it on, but I would spend, spend, spend." The judges loved Oprah's funny and truthful answer. They asked the contestants a second question: "What do you want to do with your life?"

The other teens all said they wanted to be teachers or nurses. Oprah hadn't really decided what she wanted to be. But she figured she had to say something different from everyone else. That morning she had seen broadcast journalist Barbara Walters on TV's *Today Show*. A broadcast journalist is someone who reports news stories for radio or television.

Barbara Walters was the first woman to anchor, or lead, the news on a major U.S. TV network.

"I want to be a broadcast journalist because I believe in the truth," Oprah answered. "I'm interested in proclaiming the truth to the world."

The judges were impressed with Oprah. She had a winning personality. And with her intelligence, she outshined the other contestants. Oprah was crowned Miss Fire Prevention of 1971.

"I know it's not a biggie. But for me it was special," Oprah said. "I was the only black—the first black—to win the darned thing."

The people at radio station WVOL were proud of Oprah. They gave her a watch and a digital clock. Even better, they asked her if she wanted to hear how her voice sounded on tape. Oprah eagerly agreed.

Oprah had had lots of speaking experience over the years. Because of it, she sounded almost like a professional news anchor. The anchor of a news broadcast is the person who reads the news and introduces reports by other reporters. "They couldn't believe how well I read," Oprah said later. "They said, 'Come hear this girl read.' Then someone else listened, and before I knew it, there were four guys standing there listening to me read."

Oprah was only seventeen years old and still in high school. Even so, she was offered a part-time

job as a news reader. Oprah was thrilled. After
school, she hurried to the radio station to do
newscasts at 3:30 P.M. She was doing something she
liked, and she was getting paid for it!

COLLEGE BOUND

In June 1971, Oprah graduated from East High
School. A few months later, she went to college
using her Elks Club scholarship. She attended
Tennessee State University, an all-black school in
Nashville. She planned to study speech and drama.
To save money, she would continue to live with her

Oprah's senior year high
school picture, 1971

father and stepmother. She would travel the short
distance to school every day. Oprah didn't want to
give up her news reader job. So she continued to
work part-time at WVOL.

Many issues inspired strong feelings in
students. At Oprah's all-black university, many
African American students were rallying for "Black
Power." Black Power meant trying to get more
power for black Americans through political, and
sometimes violent, activism.

"It was a weird time," Oprah said later. "This
whole 'black power' movement was going on then,
but I just never had any of those angry black feelings.
Truth is, I've never felt prevented from doing
anything because I was either black or a woman."

Oprah wasn't interested in politics or
protesting. She was much more interested in
succeeding in school. She wanted to build on her
talents and move ahead with her life. That led her
classmates to dislike her. They expected black
people to be involved in protests during this highly
political time. Some students even called her an
Oreo. This is an expression for a black person who
is considered "white on the inside and black on the
outside." Oprah grew to hate college.

In 1972, Oprah entered and won her second beauty pageant, the Miss Black Nashville contest. Then she won a third pageant, Miss Black Tennessee. Oprah was surprised to win these contests. She didn't see herself as beautiful. And she downplayed her calm manner, personality, and talent.

"I did not expect to win, nor did anybody else expect me to win," she said. "And Lord, were [the other contestants] upset. I said, 'Beats me, girls, I'm as shocked as you are.'"

Being crowned Miss Black Tennessee landed Oprah a place in the Miss Black America pageant. It was held in Hollywood, California. Oprah didn't win the contest, but the experience inspired her to set her goals high and reach for her dreams.

IT'S A FACT!

While in Hollywood, Oprah visited the Walk of Fame on Hollywood Boulevard. Hundreds of golden stars, each matched with the name of a famous film or TV star, decorate the sidewalk. Oprah told her father that one day her star would sit beside the others. Oprah's father didn't laugh. He, too, knew in his heart that his daughter was going places.

PEOPLE ARE TALKING

IN COLLEGE, Oprah attended classes, studied hard, and did a lot of reading. In her job as a news reader at radio station WVOL, she gained valuable, real-life experience.

In 1973, Oprah received a phone call from a station manager at WTVF-TV, the CBS television station in Nashville. The manager told Oprah that he had heard her on the radio and was very impressed with her talent. He wanted to hire her to anchor the evening news.

Oprah couldn't believe it. They wanted to hire her as an anchor? She was only nineteen years old. Oprah didn't think she could handle both a full-time job and college. She turned down the offer.

The station manager didn't give up easily. He called Oprah two more times. He tried to talk her

Oprah landed her first television job while she was in college.

into trying out for the job. She felt confused. She thought she might rather be an actress than a broadcaster. Oprah asked one of her favorite speech professors at Tennessee State for advice.

He couldn't believe that Oprah didn't take the job right away. "I've seen some *stupid* people," he said with a laugh. "Don't you know that's *why* people go to college? So that CBS can call them?"

Oprah thought carefully about her teacher's words. She decided to try out for the job. It could be a great opportunity.

At the audition, Oprah wasn't sure how to act.
She pretended to be TV journalist Barbara Walters. "I
would sit like Barbara, or like I imagined Barbara to
sit," Oprah said later. "I'd look down at the script and
up to the camera because I thought that's what you
do, how you act. You try to have as much eye contact
as you can—at least it seemed that way from what I
had seen Barbara do."

Oprah landed the job.
She was excited about her
salary—$15,000 a year. It
was a lot of money to her
at the time, as much as her
father was making as a
barber. Best of all, she
didn't have to quit school.
She could go to classes
during the day and work
in the evening.

At that time,
companies in the United
States had to follow new
"affirmative action"
guidelines set up by the
government. Businesses

IT'S A FACT!

Oprah wasn't only a
black employee, she
was also a woman.
Affirmative action
tries to bring not
only more African
Americans but more
women into business.
A station's broadcast
license could be held
up for not having
enough affirmative
action hirings. In
hiring Oprah, WTVF-
TV got two
affirmative action
credits for the price
of one hire.

had to ensure that a certain number of the employees they hired were minorities, such as African Americans or Asians. Some critics accused Oprah of being a "token" at the station, just filling the role of black person. Oprah didn't care if she was the station's token black or not. She was happy with her new job, and she knew she was good at it. She was the first black newscaster in Nashville history. She was also the youngest.

LEARNING THE ROPES

Oprah's first year as a TV news anchor had its ups and downs. One evening during a live newscast, Oprah made her first big "on-the-air" mistake.

"I was doing a list of foreign countries. . . . And I called Canada 'ca-NAD-a,' recalled Oprah. "I got so tickled. 'That wasn't ca-NAD-a. That was CAN-ada.' And then I started laughing. Well, it became the first real moment I ever had. And the news director later said to me, 'If you do that, then you should just keep going, you shouldn't correct yourself and let people know.' So that was, for me, the beginning of realizing, 'Oh, you can laugh at yourself, and you can make a mistake, and it's not the end of the world.' You don't have to be perfect—the biggest lesson for me for television."

Oprah didn't have to be perfect, but she did want to do her best. She studied tapes of news broadcasts she had done to find ways to improve her news delivery. She worked on her timing, rhythm, and ease in front of the camera. Soon she had developed her own warm, casual style. And she didn't copy Barbara Walters anymore.

After gaining experience at WTVF-TV, Oprah knew she wanted to continue her career in television broadcasting. She began to look around for a better broadcasting job. She sent tapes of herself to stations in big cities like New York and Los Angeles.

In 1976, Oprah received a tempting job offer. It was at WJZ-TV in Baltimore, Maryland. The job was as a news reporter and anchor. The station managers wanted her to start soon—in three months.

Oprah took some time to think it over. If she left Nashville, she'd be leaving her father and stepmother's home. She would also have to drop out of college just a few months short of graduating.

But Oprah was used to fast, big changes in her life. And she was determined to move forward with her career. The new job would be an upward move. It would mean a pay increase and a position at an important television station. Oprah decided to accept the job.

HELLO, BALTIMORE

Twenty-two-year-old Oprah arrived in Baltimore in June 1976. She couldn't wait to start her new job. Meanwhile, she rented her first apartment, shopped for new work clothes, and explored Baltimore. It was a large, bustling city.

On August 16, 1976, Oprah made her first appearance on the six o'clock news at WJZ-TV. For the show, she wore a bright red suit. Her hair was styled in a "natural," or Afro, a popular hairstyle at the time.

Unlike many young people who are starting a new job, Oprah was calm and confident. Her years of public speaking and her anchoring experience made her comfortable in front of the cameras.

IT'S A FACT

WJZ-TV placed billboards all around Baltimore to advertise Oprah's upcoming first appearance at the station. The billboards read: "WHAT'S AN OPRAH?" Oprah didn't like the billboards much.

Oprah read the news in a warm and friendly style. She came across as a real, down-to-earth person. But to some people, she was a little *too* real for the evening news. Sometimes she changed the words of the stories that she read. She wanted to make the news stories sound more casual. And she often showed personal feelings about the stories she reported.

"My openness is the reason I did not do so well as a news reporter," Oprah said. "I used to go on assignment and be so open that I would say to people at fires–and they'd lost their children– 'That's okay. You don't have to talk to me.'"

Oprah's news director wasn't as understanding. He said, "What do you mean they didn't have to talk to you?" Oprah replied, "But she just lost her child, and you know I just felt so bad."

For one assignment, Oprah was sent to report on a funeral. But she refused to go into the funeral home. She felt sorry for the families involved, and she didn't want to disturb anyone. Sometimes when Oprah was reading an especially sad story, she would even cry on the air.

Oprah's bosses didn't appreciate her natural and open style of reporting the news. In Nashville, audiences had liked her easygoing, friendly manner. But the people of Baltimore expected a more polished news anchor. Oprah didn't have the slick appearance of the other news anchors in town.

CLOUDS AND SILVER LININGS

Oprah had signed a two-year contract with the station, so the managers couldn't fire her. Instead, they took her off the evening news and gave her a five-minute time slot at 5:30 in the morning. The bosses said she had been moved because she was "so good" that she needed her own time slot. But Oprah knew better. She had been given a less important job.

"I was [deeply hurt] because up until that point, I had sort of cruised," she said. "I really hadn't thought a lot about my life, or the direction it was taking. I just happened into television, happened into radio. . . . I was twenty-two and embarrassed by the whole thing because I had never failed before."

Meanwhile, the station managers decided that Oprah needed a change in her appearance. They sent her to an expensive salon in New York to have her hair straightened and styled. Oprah wondered about their reasons for the decision. Did her bosses want her to look more like the white newscasters?

Going to the salon did not work out well. The hair stylist left the harsh straightening chemicals on for too long. They damaged Oprah's hair so badly that it fell out. She was bald for weeks and had to wear wigs.

Things didn't get better. The bosses at WJZ-TV didn't like Oprah's speaking voice, either. They had her take lessons from a professional voice coach. Oprah became depressed. Her job didn't feel right at all. But she figured she had no choice but to change the way she talked and looked. She thought it was the only way to keep her job.

IT'S A FACT!

Oprah has a round head. When she was bald, it was difficult to find a wig big enough. This fact only brought down her self-esteem even more.

She dragged herself to the voice coach's office. But, to her surprise, the coach didn't think there was anything wrong with her voice. The teacher said she just needed to learn to speak up for herself. She shouldn't let anyone try to change her into someone she wasn't. The coach warned that

Oprah would never make it in broadcasting if she didn't stand up to her bosses.

But Oprah wasn't even sure she wanted to make it in broadcasting. In her heart, she still dreamed of being an actress.

"I really don't want to do this. What I want to do is act," Oprah told the voice coach. "What I think is going to happen is that I will be discovered because I want it so badly. Somebody is going to have to discover me."

"You are a dreamer," said the coach. Oprah didn't care if she was a dreamer. She headed back to WJZ-TV with a new attitude. She would just ride this out. She would take the morning news spot and wait until something better came along.

Oprah's professional life in Baltimore was rocky, but in her personal life she made a new friend. Gayle King was another WJZ-TV newscaster. One evening, a sudden snowstorm kept Gayle from going home. Oprah invited her to stay over at her apartment, near the studio. The two bonded instantly. They delighted in the discovery that they wore the same dress and shoe size. They even had the same contact lens prescription. They soon became best friends.

Oprah found a lifelong friend in Gayle King (right).

Oprah's work life began to improve in 1978, when a new station manager was hired at WJZ-TV. He wanted Oprah to co-host a new morning talk show called *People Are Talking*. Oprah and her co-host, Richard Sher, would be interviewing famous people and some lesser-known people. The show would feature lighthearted, fun interviews as well as serious, personal stories.

The new show was a perfect fit for Oprah. "The day I did that talk show, I felt like I'd come home," she said.

She recalled, "My very first interview was the Carvel Ice Cream Man, and Benny from *All My Children*–I'll never forget it. I came off the air, thinking, 'This is what I should have been doing.'

Because it was...like breathing to me. Like breathing."

On *People Are Talking,* Oprah could be herself—warm, friendly, and funny. And viewers liked it. She loved talking with her guests about issues and feelings. And she instantly clicked with her co-host, Richard Sher. He had been a talk show host before.

At first, the management at WJZ-TV was nervous about the new show. *People Are Talking* would air during the same time slot as *The Phil Donahue Show.* Donahue was a very popular talk show host whose show was on all over the country.

But within weeks, the bosses relaxed. *People Are Talking* had a larger Baltimore audience than Donahue's show. Women viewers, especially, loved Oprah.

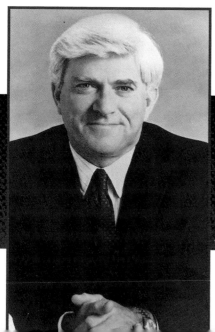

Phil Donahue was Oprah's friendly competition.

CHAPTER 8
THE OPRAH WINFREY SHOW

OPRAH CO-HOSTED the top-rated
Baltimore talk show for six years. In the fall
of 1984, when she was thirty, another big
opportunity came her way. A coworker at
WJZ-TV told her about a job opening at
WLS-TV in Chicago, Illinois. The job was
hosting a talk show called A.M. Chicago. If
Oprah landed the job, she would get a huge
pay increase.

(Above)
**Oprah
moved to
Chicago in
1984 to host
a new talk
show.**

On Labor Day, Oprah flew to Chicago, one
of the country's largest cities. She recorded a
one-hour audition tape. She spoke about herself

and a variety of topics. The station manager, Dennis Swanson, watched her audition tape in his office. Swanson walked over to Oprah and pretended to measure her head.

"*What* are you doing?" she asked.

"Your head fits very nicely on your shoulders," said Swanson. "I just want to make sure that when this great success befalls you that it [your head] will always stay there."

"Do you really think I could be that successful?" said Oprah, realizing that she had the job.

"Yes, I do," Swanson replied. He added that the station would be in contact with her soon to make a contract for her new position at *A.M. Chicago.*

Top-Rated Talker

Chicago, Illinois, is known as the Windy City on Lake Michigan. It was also the home base for Phil Donahue, Oprah's talk show rival. Could she keep up the top ratings she had scored in Baltimore?

Phil Donahue had been the first to run the type of talk show that he and Oprah did. The host takes a microphone into the audience and allows people to make comments or ask questions of the show's guests. Donahue had a simple style and talked mostly about issues instead of feelings.

Oprah, on the other hand, "got personal" on her show. She shared her own feelings, secrets, and confidence problems with her viewers. On a show about weight loss, Oprah talked about her own struggle with food. Oprah connected with her guests and her audience. When a guest was upset, Oprah usually gave her a hug or touched her hand. She was a different kind of talk show host.

IT'S A FACT!

In contrast to Phil Donahue, Oprah asked personal questions she thought everyday people would be interested in. Here's an example. Phil Donahue once interviewed Dudley Moore, a very short actor who often dated very tall women. He asked Moore about his upcoming movies. Oprah asked Moore how the short-tall dating combination worked!

Because Oprah shared her feelings, guests were inspired to talk openly about their problems, too. "My ability to get people to open up is [because] there is a common bond in the human spirit," Oprah said. "We all want the same things. And I know that."

Oprah loved her job. She didn't think things could get any better–but they did. A year after she moved to Chicago, in 1985, her show got a new name: *The Oprah Winfrey Show*. And the program soon topped *The Phil Donahue Show* in the Nielsen ratings. The Nielsen ratings are a measure of how many viewers watch a particular television show. Still, Oprah felt like something was missing in her life. She had always wanted to act in a film, not just be a TV host.

THE COLOR PURPLE

One day in 1985, a film producer and musician named Quincy Jones was in Chicago. He turned on the TV and spotted Oprah hosting her hit talk show. He knew right away that she was right for the part of Sofia in the movie he was currently producing. To produce a movie means to be the main person in charge of getting the money to make it. The movie was *The Color Purple*. Oprah had read the book earlier and had loved it.

IT'S A FACT
Some black men said that *The Color Purple* stereotyped them as always being abusive to women. They protested the movie. Some male reviewers gave it bad reviews.

DISCOVERING *THE COLOR PURPLE*

When Oprah was still in Baltimore, she was flipping through the pages of the *New York Times Book Review.* The paper had an article about a new book by an African American author named Alice Walker. The book, *The Color Purple,* was about Celie, a "poor, barely literate [able to read] Southern black woman who struggles to escape the brutality . . . of her treatment by men," the review said.

The book sounded very interesting to Oprah. After reading the review, she went out and bought the book. In fact, she bought every copy of *The Color Purple* in stock. She wanted to share it with friends.

Oprah related to Celie on a deep level because "you know that you are not the only one. Because all of this time, you have carried this burden [of abuse]. You think nobody else in the world has been through this. Nobody else is as *bad* as you. And then you discover that you are not so bad after all. It's an amazing thing."

Jones didn't waste time. He contacted the film's director, Steven Spielberg. They called Oprah and offered her the role. Oprah had been "discovered," just as she had dreamed of being for so long. She called it "absolutely divine intervention [God making something happen]." In the film, Oprah played Sofia, a woman who fights back against an abusive husband named Harpo. Harpo was played by Willard Pugh. *The Color Purple* was released in December 1985. Some reviewers liked it, but many did not. Oprah's performance, however, was praised. *Newsweek* magazine called her portrayal of Sofia a "delight."

In 1986, Oprah was nominated, or chosen as a finalist, for an Academy Award for her performance in the film. The Academy Awards are given out by the film industry every year to recognize the year's

Sofia, a character in *The Color Purple*, is a strong-willed woman who doesn't back down in the face of abuse and racism. Oprah played Sofia *(above)*.

greatest work in films. They are nicknamed the Oscars. Oprah arrived at the Oscars dressed in a beautiful, bead-trimmed, gold and ivory gown. She wore a diamond necklace and earrings. She also wore a ten-thousand-dollar fox fur coat, dyed bright purple after the movie's title. Oprah looked stunning, but she felt fat. Her dress was so tight she could hardly breathe during the ceremony.

Throughout her career, Oprah had often found comfort in food. She turned to food when she felt stressed. As a result, she had steadily put on weight. At the 1986 Academy Awards, she was almost at her heaviest point.

Oprah did not win an Oscar. Afterward, she tried to make light of her disappointment as well as her weight problems. "Perhaps God was saying to me, 'Oprah, you are not winning because your dress is too tight for you to make it up all those steps to receive the statuette,'" she told a writer for *McCall's* magazine.

Oprah tried not to be too discouraged about her loss at the Academy Awards. She knew that being nominated for an Oscar was a great honor in itself. She also knew that she wanted to continue acting in films.

Meanwhile, *The Oprah Winfrey Show* continued to receive top ratings. In 1986, Oprah signed a deal with King World Productions, Inc. King World bought the rights to national syndication (to broadcast the show to audiences all over the country). People across the United States got to know Oprah, the first African American host of a national TV talk show.

Oprah's fame soon grew enormous. In the late 1980s, she was on her way to give a speech. Her best friend, Gayle, rode in the car with her. They pulled closer to the auditorium where Oprah was to speak. The two friends could see police cars, long lines, and a big crowd of people. A traffic jam clogged the street.

"Who's coming?" asked Gayle.

"I am," said Oprah.

"No, no, I mean, who is really coming? Besides you? Who are all of these policemen for?"

"Me," said Oprah, laughing.

Gayle was shocked. "Oh, my goodness," she said. "What is becoming of you?"

HARPO PRODUCTIONS

Another good thing about national syndication was that Oprah made a lot more money—nearly

$125 million a year. With her increased income, Oprah decided to form her own production company. A production company produces, or makes, movies and television shows. She called her company Harpo Productions, Inc. Oprah became one of the first women in history to own a TV and film production company.

Through her new company, Oprah began to buy the film rights to literary works such as novels. This allowed Harpo to make movies based on those works. The company bought the film rights to several novels. These included *Their Eyes Were Watching God* by Zora Neale Hurston and *The Wedding* by Dorothy West.

IT'S A FACT!

"Harpo" is Oprah spelled backward. It is also the name of her husband's character in *The Color Purple*.

Oprah continued to work hard on her talk show. She did shows about child abuse, divorce, being overweight, and many other topics. Whatever the topic, she worked to let people know that they had the power to change their lives.

Oprah also stressed the importance of dealing with the past and healing emotional pain. "If you don't heal your personal wounds, they continue to bleed," she said. "And so we have a country of people who have continued to bleed."

In the late 1980s, *The Oprah Winfrey Show* began to change. It focused more on personal growth and spiritual growth, or growth of the soul. Oprah hosted guests such as inspirational speaker Marianne Williamson. Williamson encouraged people to reach for their best selves.

Oprah agreed with Williamson's ideas. "As a kid . . . I always wanted to be a minister and preach," said Oprah. "And I think, in many ways, that I have been able to fulfill all of that. I feel that my show is a ministry [place where preaching and ministering are done]."

But Oprah isn't just a speaker. "She does something that most people don't

Quincy Jones and Oprah on the set of *The Color Purple*

have a clue about," said Quincy Jones. "She knows
how to listen. And she listens not just with her
head. She listens with her heart and soul."

In 1987, Oprah accepted her first Daytime
Emmy Award, for Outstanding Talk Show Host.
Emmys are awarded every year to recognize the
year's best work in television. Oprah's show also
won Emmys for Best Talk Show and Best Talk
Show Director.

LOVE IN THE AIR

Oprah's TV and film career was going great. But
her personal life lacked romance. That changed in
1987. She met a man who would stay by her side
for years to come.

Stedman Graham was good looking and tall. He
was a former model and basketball player. He worked
as the executive director of a nonprofit program
called Athletes Against Drugs. He had been married
once and had a young daughter, Wendy. Oprah had
met Stedman at fund-raisers and parties around
Chicago. But she had never spent time with him.

One day, Stedman called Oprah and asked her
for a date. Oprah thought he seemed nice, and she
liked him. But she was afraid that Stedman liked

her just because she was famous and wealthy. So she turned him down. Stedman was determined, however. He called Oprah several times, each time asking her for a date. Finally, she gave in and went out with him. Within weeks, their dating turned into a serious, committed relationship.

Oprah took an important step in her career in 1988. Harpo Productions bought the rights to *The Oprah Winfrey Show*. Oprah had the power to produce her own show her own way. She planned to start doing pretaped shows instead of live ones. That would give her more flexibility and free time in her schedule. She also wanted to find a new studio for the show and nicer, more comfortable surroundings for her staff.

IT'S A FACT!

In 1988, Oprah won the International Radio and Television Society's award. She was named Broadcaster of the Year. She was the youngest ever to win and only the fifth woman to win.

She was thinking big. She spent $10 million on an 88,000-square-foot production studio. It was a half-mile west of downtown Chicago and as long as a city block. She then laid down another $10 million to remodel the building. She added a TV studio, staff gym, and fancy offices. She added a movie screening room complete with a popcorn machine. She named the new studio Harpo Studios.

Oprah's empire–the companies she owned and controlled–continued to grow. In 1989, she opened a restaurant with a man named Richard Melman, who had run many restaurants in Chicago. The unusual restaurant was called the Eccentric. It featured the food and look of four different countries–the United States, England, France, and Italy. The American menu included some of

Located on Erie Street in downtown Chicago, the Eccentric was one of the city's hot spots.

Stedman Graham is originally from Whitesboro, New Jersey. He played professional basketball in Europe before returning to the United States and entering the business world.

Oprah's favorite dishes. One dish was "Oprah's Potatoes," made with potatoes, horseradish, parsley, and cream.

Oprah's power and fame became greater and greater. As it did, the media seemed to bully her more and more. The media are newspapers, magazines, radio and television stations, and other places people get news and information. Oprah and Stedman were very happy together, but the media wouldn't leave them alone. "Why aren't you married?" reporters repeatedly asked. The media wrote mean-spirited stories suggesting that Stedman only stayed with Oprah for her money. Tabloid newspapers, such as the *National Enquirer,* were the meanest.

Sometimes the press made rude comments about Oprah's weight. She was deeply upset by the articles. "The tabloids used to make me cry all the time," she said. "Every time they would come out with the least little thing about me, I used to [cry]."

WEIGHT ISSUES

The stories were all the more painful because Oprah badly wanted to lose weight. In 1988, during the summer break from her show, she went on a strict liquid diet. For three and a half months, she ate nothing but a particular diet drink. Because the diet was so extreme, a doctor carefully watched her progress. Oprah also started working out at a gym and jogging.

Oprah in Los Angeles, California. Her popularity was growing but so was her struggle with her weight.

She had lost sixty-seven pounds by the time the fall television season began.

On November 15, 1988, Oprah shared her weight-loss victory with her viewers. She came onstage dressed in tight-fitting, size 10 designer jeans. She pulled a wagon filled with sixty-seven pounds of animal fat. The animal fat represented the weight she had lost. The audience clapped and cheered Oprah's success.

Other viewers were not as happy about her newly thin figure. Many people admired Oprah Winfrey because

Oprah after losing sixty-seven pounds

she could be so successful *without* being thin. What message was she sending now about body image? Some viewers felt that Oprah had let them down.

But Oprah wasn't happy being overweight. She wanted to lose weight for herself more than for anyone else. She felt healthier and more sure of herself. Unfortunately, Oprah gained the weight back quickly. This is common for people who follow rapid weight-loss programs.

Oprah's ups and downs on the scale did not slow her career success. Her show continued to pick up top ratings and several awards. Still, the tabloid press continued to give her a hard time. It had been three years since Oprah and Stedman got together. Rumors got started that Stedman was gay.

"That was the most difficult time for me," said Oprah. "I believe in my heart that had I not been an overweight woman, that rumor would never have occurred. If I were lean and pretty, nobody would ever say that. What people were really saying is why would a straight, good-looking guy be with her?"

"He was so brave," Oprah added. "And I never loved him more. He taught me so much during that period. When I handed [the article] to him, he looked at it and said, 'This is not my life. I don't have anything to do with this.'"

Oprah was learning the huge challenges of being famous. She couldn't walk alone with Stedman at a park, for example, without photographers following them. In 1989, Oprah bought a 160-acre farm in Rolling Prairie, Indiana. The farm was a place to get away from the pressure of being famous. The property included an eight-room guesthouse. It also had a charming log cabin, a gym, a pool, and a barn with nine horses.

"I've never loved a place the way I love my farm," Oprah told a writer for *Essence* magazine. "I grew up in the country, which is probably why I'm so attached to the land. . . . I love the lay of the land. I love walking the land. And I love knowing that it's my land."

Oprah liked spending time on her farm because she could unwind there and be herself. She didn't have to be "on"–smiling for the cameras. Underneath her stardom, she was a regular person, with problems like anyone else. In 1989, her brother Jeffrey died of AIDS. Oprah had not been in close contact with Jeffrey or other members of her family over the years. Still, his death hit her hard.

Oprah hasn't talked publicly much about her family members or her relationship with them. Oprah says her grandmother, Hattie Mae Lee, shaped her life the most of all her relatives. "My grandmother gave me the foundation for success that I was allowed to continue to build upon," Oprah said. "My grandmother taught me to read, and that opened the door to all kinds of possibilities for me."

7 NEW DIRECTIONS

IN 1990, one episode of Oprah's show changed the way she looked at herself. She was interviewing a woman who had been severely abused as a child. Because of her abuse, the woman had serious mental health problems. While listening to the woman's story, Oprah thought, "'Oh, that's why I was that way.' I always blamed myself. Even though ... I would speak to people and say, 'Oh, the child's never to blame. You're never responsible for the molestation in your life.' I still believed I was responsible somehow. That I was a bad girl.

"So it happened on the air, as so many things happen for me. It happened on the air in the middle of someone else's experience, and I thought I was going to have a breakdown on television. And I said, 'Stop! Stop! You've got to stop rolling cameras!' And they didn't, so I got myself through it, but it was really quite [upsetting] for me.

"And I realize that I was the kind of child who was always searching for love and affection and attention, and somebody to . . . look at me and say, 'Yes, you are worthy [valuable].' Unfortunately, there are adults who will take advantage of that and misread your intentions."

The show was a turning point for Oprah. From then on, she tried to overcome her need to be a "people pleaser." She worked to change her old pattern of wanting everyone to like her. She was determined not to let her childhood abuse keep hurting her.

Oprah realized that she could use her painful past in a positive way. She could help other victims of abuse. "A part of my mission in life now is to encourage every other child who has been abused to tell. You tell, and if they don't believe you, you keep telling," Oprah said. "You tell everybody until somebody listens to you."

IT'S A FACT!

In 1993, President Bill Clinton signed into law the National Child Protection Act. It was more popularly known as Oprah's Bill.

In 1991, Oprah told the nation's lawmakers about her abuse. She spoke before the U.S. Senate Judiciary Committee. She worked to get a new law passed, the National Child Protection Act. The act established a nationwide database of convicted child abusers.

TAKING CONTROL

In June 1992, Oprah accepted her third Daytime Emmy Award for Outstanding Talk Show Host. But she wasn't happy. She said she was embarrassed at having to "waddle my way up to the stage with the nation watching my huge behind." Oprah's weight had climbed to an all-time high of 237 pounds. "I felt like such a loser, like I'd lost control of my life," she remembered. "I was the fattest woman in the room."

For Oprah, overeating was caused by uncomfortable feelings. These feelings included nervousness, sadness, and

Oprah with her third Daytime Emmy Award for Outstanding Talk Show Host

fear. After the Emmy Awards, Oprah went to a spa in Telluride, Colorado, to lose weight. There she met personal trainer Bob Greene. Oprah liked Greene right away. He was warm and friendly. And he didn't have a TV, so he didn't know much about her. Oprah asked Greene to develop a fitness program for her.

Oprah lost more than ten pounds at the spa, thanks to eating a low-fat diet and following Greene's exercise program. She felt better than she had in years. Oprah talked Bob Greene into moving to Chicago to be her personal trainer. His job would be to help her get in shape. Greene took the job.

Oprah and her trainer, Bob Greene

Greene made sure that Oprah began her fitness program slowly. At first, she walked each day. She worked her way up to jogging three miles a day, then eight miles a day. She worked out six days a week. When she went on vacation, Greene went with her. He was as dedicated to Oprah's fitness as she was. A few months later, Oprah completed a thirteen-mile race in San Diego, California.

The main goal of her new fitness program was good health, not just losing weight. She also got support from her personal chef, Rosie Daley. Daley kept Oprah on a diet of delicious, low-fat food. By 1993, Oprah had lost almost ninety pounds.

Meanwhile, Oprah continued to have great success with her show. Every television season, it was the number-one rated talk show. Millions of people around the United States watched it. Millions more tuned in worldwide.

IT'S A FACT!

On February 10, 1993, Oprah interviewed the singer Michael Jackson. Jackson is famous for disliking to be personally interviewed. About 62 million people—a bit more than the entire population of France—tuned in to this one show.

HELPING OTHERS

In 1994, Oprah and Daley published *In the Kitchen with Rosie*. It was a cookbook of low-fat recipes by Daley. The day after Oprah talked about the book on her show, it sold at a record-breaking rate. It remained a best-seller for almost a year.

Oprah found joy in helping others to achieve success. In 1993, Deepak Chopra, a doctor from India, appeared on Oprah's show. Soon after, Chopra's book *Ageless Body, Timeless Mind* shot to the top of the best-seller lists.

In 1994, Oprah found a different way to help people. She hosted a charity event, an event to raise money for people in need. Her event was an auction of fancy clothing and shoes she had worn. It was held at Chicago's Hyatt Regency Hotel.

IT'S A FACT!

One of Oprah's nicknames is Deepak Oprah. This is a word play on Deepak Chopra, whom she admires.

One woman who went to the auction was a poor, single mother. She could only afford a five-dollar pair of shoes that were size ten. She wouldn't be able to wear the shoes, since her feet were size seven. But she wanted the shoes anyway. Later, the woman met Oprah after attending one of her shows. She told Oprah, "Sometimes I go in the closet when I'm feeling down and I stand in your shoes." "That story makes me want to weep," said Oprah. "It makes me think I must be doing something right."

The ratings for *The Oprah Winfrey Show* continued to be high. Still, Oprah looked for ways to make her show even better. She was tired of doing shows about damaged families, fighting relatives, and messed-up lives.

"I was in the middle of a show with some [racist people such as] white supremacists, skinheads, Ku Klux Klan members," Oprah remembered, "and I just had a flash, I thought, 'This is doing nobody any good—nobody.' I had [told myself], 'Oh, people need to know that these kinds of people are out here.' I won't do it anymore."

Oprah preferred to uplift and inspire viewers. In May 1995, she launched a six-week series on her show called "Get Movin' with Oprah." With the series, she hoped to help viewers get into fitness and exercise.

OPRAH'S BOOK CLUB

She also wanted to share her love of books with her viewers. "What a difference it makes in your world to go into some other life. It's what I love most. I'm reading always to leave myself . . . behind," said Oprah. "That's what reading is. You get to leave."

SOME OF OPRAH'S FAVORITE AUTHORS

Oprah has been a thirsty reader her entire life. She has long been drawn to female characters who get through hard times. Some of her favorite authors include:

Maya Angelou (born 1928), the author of *I Know Why the Caged Bird Sings*. This first part of Angelou's autobiography traces her life in the 1930s and 1940s. Although Angelou begins as an insecure girl, she experiences many trials that make her into a self-assured young woman.

Toni Morrison (born 1931), the author of *Beloved*. This dark and powerful novel addresses the long-term effects of slavery on a woman named Sethe. Oprah played Sethe in the 1998 movie version.

Alice Walker (born 1944), the author of *The Color Purple*. This novel describes the pain suffered by Celie, the main character and her transformation. Another character, Sofia, doesn't back down from racism and abuse. Oprah played Sofia in the movie version.

Margaret Walker (1915–1998), the author of *Jubilee*. This story about a slave named Vyry before, during, and after the Civil War shares the details of black life in the South. Despite much suffering, Vyry survives and forgives those who have hurt her.

In 1996, Oprah started a reading group, Oprah's Book Club. On her show, she assigned a book for viewers to read. A month later, book club members would tune in for a talk with the author of the book.

Oprah's first book club selection was *The Deep End of the Ocean*. The novel is about a family learning to live with the disappearance of a child. The book's author was Jacquelyn Mitchard. Mitchard saw that many of the books—and authors—later chosen for the book club had things in common. "All of the authors that she has picked for the book club were lonely children whose refuge was in books," Mitchard remarked. "Oprah is clearly in that club."

Oprah's Book Club was a hit right from the start. It helped boost the show's audience to nearly twenty million viewers. And the viewers bought the books that Oprah recommended. Book sales soared. The popularity of book clubs increased, too. People across the country formed their own book clubs.

Book publishers were not prepared at first for the huge demand created by Oprah's show. The huge sales caused by Oprah's show was called the Oprah phenomenon. It was the biggest change to hit the publishing industry in fifteen years, according to Philip Pfeffer. Pfeffer is the chief executive officer of the Borders bookstore chain. "Oprah Winfrey has been able to generate [create] interest in reading through her book club," Pfeffer said. "The thing that's amazing to me is *Oprah Winfrey* airs at 4 p.m. The show is not watched by what we consider our [regular customers]. But Oprah's viewers go out and buy the books featured on the show."

Oprah also asked well-known writers to be part of the book club. These writers included Toni Morrison, the author of award-winning books such as *Song of Solomon* and *Beloved*. Oprah called Morrison "the greatest living American writer, male or female, white or black."

Oprah greatly admires Toni Morrison.

Oprah poses with the book she coauthored with her trainer.

In 1996, Oprah talked about a book on her show that she herself had a part in creating. The book was *Make the Connection: Ten Steps to a Better Body—and a Better Life.* In it, Oprah discusses her struggles with weight loss. She and her personal trainer Bob Greene, describe a day-by-day fitness plan, using a positive, self-loving approach.

"I love this book because for so many years I struggled and wanted to be Diana Ross," Oprah said. "Then I realized no matter what I did I was not gonna have Diana's thighs! I realized that I just have to settle into what is the best body for me."

Oprah was learning to love herself more–and feel joy in her life. "I used to say I didn't have time to experience joy. I had too much to do," she said. "But I started to be aware of the life I'm living. . . . Now when we're running, I smell the jasmine; I notice when there's a pack of butterflies."

8 A WOMAN WITH WINGS

(Above) Lots of good things were happening in Oprah's life in the late 1990s.

IN 1997, Oprah started Oprah's Angel Network. The goal of this charity was simply to make the world a better place to live. It would give college scholarships to fifty young people a year, chosen by the Boys and Girls Clubs of America. Each young person receives a $25,000 college scholarship.

Oprah also asked viewers to create their own "mini-miracle." They could do this by donating their spare change to the "world's largest piggy bank." With the money, Oprah planned to build more than two hundred "Oprah Houses" for Habitat for Humanity. Habitat for Humanity is a group that helps poor families build good houses. The houses are priced low enough that the families can own them.

IT'S A FACT!
By the summer of 2000, Oprah's Angel Network had collected more than $35 million.

Oprah's efforts continued in 1997. Harpo began production on a series of high-quality made-for-television movies titled *Oprah Winfrey Presents.* Harpo Productions would broadcast the TV films over the next three years.

The first of these movies was *Before Women Had Wings*. It showed in November 1997. The film is based on the novel by Connie May Fowler. It stars Oprah Winfrey and Ellen Barkin. It is about a poor, abused girl named Bird Johnson. A few months later, in February 1998, *The Wedding* aired. Another film in the series was *Tuesdays with Morrie,* the true story of a man's weekly visits with his dying former teacher.

Also in 1997, Oprah released a videotape version of the book *Making the Connection*. It was called *Oprah: Make the Connection*. She said the video was "about how to take control of your life. I am now about trying to convince people to stop wasting time. I know it's hard because it's much easier to want to believe there's some kind of magic fix coming along."

Oprah was always looking for ways to make her talk show more lively and interesting. In mid-1997, she made an announcement to her TV audience. She said that she would be taping an upcoming Oprah's

It's a Fact

People magazine chose Oprah as one of the 50 Most Beautiful People in the World in 1997.

Maya Angelou *(left)* and Oprah have become great friends.

Book Club show at the home of poet and novelist
Maya Angelou. Angelou had recently released a new
nonfiction book, *The Heart of a Woman.* Oprah has
called her "the woman who has had, undoubtedly,
the greatest influence on my life."

Oprah had forgotten to "OK" the book club
party beforehand. When Oprah made the
announcement, Maya was watching the show at
home. She started laughing. She shouted at the
television, "But you haven't spoken to me!" [84]

Oprah won her over. In June 1997, Maya
threw an on-the-air Book Club pajama party at her
home in Winston-Salem, North Carolina. Maya,
Oprah, and four other women, all wearing comfy
pajamas, discussed *The Heart of a Woman.*
Afterward, Maya served a big, home-cooked meal.

TROUBLE IN TEXAS

Oprah worked hard to make her show full of
useful information. After a while, that got her in
trouble. The episode of *The Oprah Winfrey Show*
that aired on April 16, 1996, was called
"Dangerous Food." On the show, Oprah's guests
talked about the risks of mad cow disease. This
rare disease affects the brain. It was said to come

from eating beef. At the time, there had not been a case of it in the United States.

At one point in the show, a vegetarian activist talked about the dangers of the disease. Oprah blurted out, "It has just stopped me cold from eating another burger."

Oprah's comment made some people very angry, especially a group of Texas cattle ranchers. They filed a lawsuit against Oprah. They claimed that her words had harmed their image. They said her statement had cost the cattle industry millions of dollars.

In January 1998, Oprah traveled to Amarillo, Texas, for the trial. She brought her staff from Harpo Productions with her. Oprah appeared in court every day for the trial, then taped her talk show after leaving the courthouse.

Oprah remained calm throughout the trial. After six weeks, the Texas jury found that Oprah was not responsible for damage to the beef industry. All charges against her were dropped.

"Free speech not only lives, it rocks!" Oprah happily announced at the end of the trial. "I will continue to use my voice," she said. "I believed from the beginning that this was an attempt to muzzle

A joyful Oprah celebrates in Amarillo, Texas, after winning the lawsuit brought against her by cattle ranchers.

[cover up] that voice. And I come from a people who have struggled and died in order to have a voice in this country, and I refuse to be muzzled."

BELOVED

Oprah has always felt a strong sense of pride in her heritage, the traditions handed down by generations of African Americans. In 1997, she started a new project that meant a lot to her. She would star in the movie version of *Beloved*, a novel by Toni Morrison.

The film was directed by Jonathan Demme. Oprah played Sethe, an escaped slave living on a farm in Ohio in 1873. Sethe is haunted by her memories of being a slave on the Sweet Home plantation. She is also haunted by the ghost of her baby daughter, Beloved. Sethe is reunited with another ex-slave from Sweet Home, Paul D, played by Danny Glover.

Oprah knew that making the film wasn't going to be easy. But she didn't know just how hard it

Oprah played Sethe in *Beloved* along with Danny Glover (*right*), who played Paul D.

would be to play the role of Sethe. She struggled to understand the feelings that come from slavery.

"I thought I knew it," she said. But she didn't understand the feelings as well as she thought she did. "During the process of doing *Beloved*, for the first time, I went to the knowing place," she said.

Oprah wanted to prepare for her film role and get a closer sense of what it was like to be a slave. She was dumped at a spot in the Maryland woods. The spot used to be part of the Underground Railroad, a route that runaway slaves had traveled to escape slavery. White men acting the part of slave trackers called her names. Oprah felt strong and unafraid at first. But then she broke down.

"I became hysterical," Oprah said. "It was raw, raw, raw pain," Oprah went on. "I went to the darkest place, and I saw the light. And I thought, 'So this is where I come from.'"

The experience of making *Beloved* stayed with Oprah long after filming was over. "The first time I saw [the film], I thought they were going to have to carry me out," she said. "Every single image caused such intense, deeply felt emotions."

Beloved was released in movie theaters in October 1998. While the film received good reviews, it did not sell many tickets. Oprah was disappointed that so few people went to the movie. But she had grown as a person by making the movie. She had also formed a solid bond with the book's author, Toni Morrison. Oprah invited her friend to her farm in Indiana.

Morrison was impressed by Oprah's book-filled home. "Except for other writers', I have very seldom [rarely] seen a home with so many books–all kinds of books, handled and read books," said Morrison.

Besides reading, Oprah enjoyed spending time with friends and with Stedman. "I decided that I wanted to have more fun in my life, and I've been having a ball," she said in 1998.

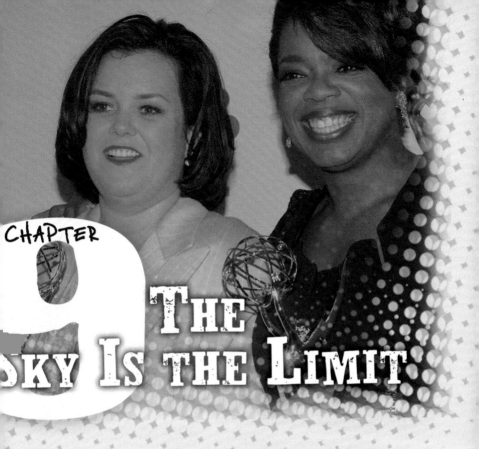

CHAPTER 9

THE SKY IS THE LIMIT

OPRAH AND *The Oprah Winfrey Show* had been winning Daytime Emmy Awards almost every year. In 1998, Oprah received a Daytime Emmy Award for lifetime achievement. She decided that she would take her name off the Daytime Emmy Award list forever. She figured that there wasn't much left after winning a lifetime award.

In the fall of 1998, Oprah began a new season of her show. She called the new season *Change Your Life TV*. One guest was John

(Above)
Oprah and Rosie O'Donnell show off the Daytime Emmy Awards they won in 1998.

Gray, author of the best-selling self-help book *Men Are from Mars, Women Are from Venus.* Gray stresses that men and women handle emotions differently. On the show, he encouraged couples to work out their problems in helpful, useful, creative ways. Oprah also added a new part to the show called "Remembering Your Spirit." In it, she showed how viewers could take time for themselves. She talked about how people could take care of their spiritual lives, or the lives of their souls.

Millions of viewers, mostly women, tune in to *The Oprah Winfrey Show* each week. It remains the highest-rated talk show in history. About twenty-five thousand letters and e-mails arrive at Harpo Productions each week. *The Oprah Winfrey Show* is seen in 119 countries, including South Africa, China, Japan, and Israel. Oprah is the wealthiest female entertainer in the world.

IT'S A FACT!

In Great Britain, Oprah's selected reruns are called *Oprah Gold.*

STAYING CENTERED

How does Oprah handle the pressures of fame and success? She starts each day with quiet meditation—

focusing her mind. Oprah's routine also includes daily exercise for her body. In the city, she uses treadmill and stairmaster exercise machines. But when she's at her farm in Indiana, she likes to hike or jog in the fields or swim in her pool. On her days off, Oprah likes to stay at her farm and read, relax, and play with her dogs.

Stedman is still a big part of Oprah's life. He continues to provide a lot of support, "not only in our relationship, but also as a trusted advisor," she says.

Oprah gets a hug from her longtime boyfriend, Stedman.

In June 1999, Oprah and Stedman taught a business course together. It was held at Northwestern University's Kellogg Graduate School of Management. The course, "Dynamics of Leadership," was held one night a week for ten weeks. "It has always been a dream of mine to teach," said Oprah. "When Stedman invited me to be a part of his class, I jumped at the opportunity."

MEDIA SUPERWOMAN

Oprah tried something new in January 2000. Harpo joined TV production company Carsey-Werner-Mandabach. They formed a new cable television network, the Oxygen Network, for women of all ages. Harpo's *Online with Oprah* at <www.oprah.com> is related to to the Oxygen channel. More than one million people visit oprah.com each day.

"It's an extension of who I am and what I want to be in the world," says Oprah of the Oxygen Network. "[We've] created a wonderful platform to bring women to themselves as best we know how. There's not better work. Sometimes we get giddy."

Oprah gets her picture taken with a fan.

Newsweek calls Oprah Winfrey "one of the most powerful brand names in the entertainment industry"—meaning that anything with the name Oprah on it is bound to be a success.

What hasn't Oprah done? In May 2000, she teamed up with Hearst Magazines to start yet another new project—her own magazine. *O: The Oprah Magazine* features upbeat self-improvement articles and inspirational stories. The first issue of *O* came out in mid-2000. It sold 1.1 million copies.

Oprah demands perfection from the *O* staff. "Look," she told the staff. "I know that to you guys the Oprah name is a brand. But for me, it's my life . . . and the way I behave and everything I stand for."

Each month, Oprah writes a column for the magazine. In the first issue, she wrote about her mission for the magazine. "How far can you grow?" she wrote. "What will it take for you to fulfill your potential [be the best you can be]? My hope is that this magazine will help you lead a more productive life."

Some critics say that Oprah acts too much like a preacher or a psychologist on her show and in the magazine. But millions of people continue to seek inspiration from Oprah. In June 2000, Oprah held her Personal Growth Summit. She brought the self-help seminar to four cities. "I'm not here to preach to anyone about how to run your life," she told one crowd. "I just know what worked for me and I'm here to share it."

"Oprah is a good mentor [guide] for us black women," said Janet Graham, a woman who had gone to a seminar. She was a thirty-six-year-old counselor for abused women and children. "She's been through a lot and nothing's been handed to her. . . . It's inspiring. How big do you dream, especially if you've

never seen anyone who looks like you reach that
high? Because of her, other women reach higher."

Oprah continues to give not only her time to
people, but her money as well. In July 2000, she
wrote a check for $10 million to A Better Chance.
The organization places
gifted minority students in
top schools across the
country. In 2002, she gave
50,000 Christmas gifts to
kids in South Africa, a
country recovering from
years of harsh
government. She later
started working on
building schools there.

Oprah still struggles
with very human issues,
even though her career has
been a huge success. One

IT'S A FACT!

After the terrorist
attacks of September
11, 2001, Oprah led an
interfaith meeting (a
meeting of people
from many different
religions). It was to
honor and remember
those who died in
the attacks. The huge
crowd filled up
Yankee Stadium in
New York.

issue is her weight. "I eat when I'm happy, I eat
when I'm sad, I eat when I'm depressed," Oprah
says. "I eat when I can't decide am I happy,
depressed or sad. I say, 'Let me have some potato
chips and decide.'"

Oprah's money doesn't protect her from problems. "I am so rich I cannot believe it," Oprah said at a Personal Growth Summit meeting. But, she added, "Every issue y'all have had, I've had it too."

Oprah's energy seemed to run low in 2002. In March of that year, she said she would stop doing her show after the 2005–2006 season. The next month she stopped doing her book club. However, in May 2003, she signed a contract to continue doing *The Oprah Winfrey Show* through the 2007–2008 season. In June 2003, she started the book club again. And she added the start of a new part of her show called *Oprah after the Show*. It is an informal time for the audience and the guests to talk.

IT'S A FACT!

In 2003, *Forbes* magazine listed Oprah Winfrey as the first African American woman to become a billionaire.

Oprah does not get too proud. She doesn't see herself as a leader or a preacher or a teacher anymore. At heart, she doesn't think she's different from anyone else.

"I'm just a voice trying to help people rediscover their best selves," she says. "All of us

OPRAH'S 50TH BIRTHDAY BASH

On January 29, 2004, during a special live edition of her show, Oprah began a weekend-long birthday celebration. She was turning fifty with Gayle and a lot of her longtime friends.

On the show, actor John Travolta acted as host. Oprah was made to sit in the audience. Singers Tina Turner and Stevie Wonder performed. Former South African president Nelson Mandela sent a taped message of admiration. Fellow talk-show host Jay Leno wheeled in a huge birthday cake.

This event was followed by a private bash at a ranch in California. Actors Halle Berry, Tom Hanks, Jennifer Aniston, and Brad Pitt were among the two hundred invited guests. As Oprah later described it, "It was the most glamorous, extravagant, fabulous thing anybody had ever seen!"

Oprah celebrates her birthday with (from left to right) Stevie Wonder, John Travolta, Gayle King, and Tina Turner.

have that within us. [It's like] *The Wizard of Oz,* when Glinda, the Good Witch, tells Dorothy, 'You've always had it, my dear.' You've always had the power. Everyone has the power inside."

GLOSSARY

affirmative action: a U.S. government effort to improve the chances that a minority person or a woman can get a good job and a good education

Baptist: a member of a large Protestant Christian group that believes only mature church members can make the decision to be baptized (or to join the church)

black power: a point of view that formed in the 1960s to push for African Americans to create their own political, economic, and cultural systems

Boys and Girls Clubs of America: a not-for-profit youth group that tries to help kids from low-income backgrounds

cable television: a television service in which signals from television stations are sent into the homes of paying customers by way of a cable or wire

civil rights movement: a group that joins together to push for freedom and equal treatment of all members of society under the law

co-host: to be in charge of a TV show, radio show, or other entertainment with another person

Elks Club: an American charity that gives millions of dollars to study kid-related diseases and to send kids to college

Habitat for Humanity: a Christian, not-for-profit group that builds quality, low-cost housing in the United States and around the world for people of any—or no—religion

mad cow disease: a fatal brain illness in cattle that can be picked up by humans who eat beef containing the disease

media: newspapers, television, radio, and the Internet that are used to get information to a large number of people at once

meditation: a way of relaxing the body and mind

national syndication: a means of selling TV programs directly to local stations throughout the United States

Nielsen ratings: a system developed by Nielsen Media Research to find out which shows TV viewers watch at what times. The higher the rating—meaning the more people who watch—the more a network can charge for advertising.

plantation: a large farm usually in a warm climate. In the 1700s and up to the mid-1800s, plantations in the southern United States typically used slave labor.

racial prejudice: an opinion formed unfairly about an ethnic group. Racial prejudice can lead to racial segregation, or the practice of keeping ethnic groups apart.

the South: in the United States, the states that fought against the Union (or North) in the Civil War (1861–1865). Oprah's home state of Mississippi is part of the South.

tabloid: a newspaper that has short articles and many pictures. The goal of most tabloid newspapers is to stir up gossip.

Underground Railroad: a network of people in the 1850s and 1860s who secretly helped slaves from the South escape to freedom in the North or in Canada

U.S. Senate Judiciary Committee: a group of senators who have a say in how the country's legal courts work

U.S. Supreme Court: the highest court in the United States. Decisions made by judges on the U.S. Supreme Court affect the entire country.

women's rights movement: a group that joined together to push for equal rights for women in every area of life

SOURCE NOTES

4 "Oprah Winfrey:
Entertainment
Executive," *Academy of
Achievement: Oprah
Winfrey Interview,*
February 21, 1991, <http
://www.achievement.org
/autodoc/page/win0int-
1> (June 4, 2004).

8 Ron Stodghill, "Daring
to Go There," *Time,*
October 5, 1998, 80.

9 "Oprah Winfrey:
Entertainment
Executive."

9 Ibid.

9 Marilyn Johnson,
"Oprah Winfrey," *Life,*
September 1997, 44.

11 Audreen Buffalo, *Meet
Oprah Winfrey* (New
York: Random House,
1993), 27–28.

12 Johnson, 44.

13 Jenny Allen, "Oprah
Winfrey," *US Weekly,*
June 12, 2000, 67.

16 Johnson, 44.

16 "Oprah Winfrey:
Entertainment
Executive."

17 Ibid.

20 "That's the Wonderful
Thing about Great
Teachers: Every One Is
an Inspiration to
Somebody," *CTA
Quest,* n.d., <http
://www.ctaquest.org
/quest_quest/1_oprah
/oprah.html>
(September 1, 2000).

21 John Culhane, "Oprah
Winfrey: How Truth
Changed Her Life,"
Reader's Digest,
February 1989, 102.

23 Johnson, 44.

24 "Oprah Winfrey:
Entertainment
Executive."

25 Norman King,
Everybody Loves Oprah
(New York: William
Morrow and Co.,
1987), 48.

26 Ibid., 49.

31 Culhane, 103.

30–33 Johnson, 44.

33 King, 62.

35 "Oprah Winfrey:
Entertainment
Executive."

35 Ibid.

36 Ibid.

37 Ibid.

37 King, 63.

37 "Oprah Winfrey:
Entertainment
Executive."

39 King, 75.

40 Audrey Edwards,
"Oprah Winfrey,
Stealing the Show,"
Essence, October 1986,
52.

42 King, 78

43 Ibid., 79.

44–45 "Oprah Winfrey:
Entertainment
Executive."

47 Ibid.

48 Ibid.
50 Ibid.
51 Allen, 67.
51–52 "Oprah Winfrey: Entertainment Executive."
57 Johnson, 44.
57 "Oprah Winfrey: Entertainment Executive."
53 *Oprah Winfrey: Heart of the Matter*, prod. Eileen Lucas, 120 minutes, ABC News Productions for A&E Networks, © 1999 ABC Inc. and A&E Networks, videocassette.
54 Ibid.
55 "Oprah Winfrey: Entertainment Executive."
56–57 Johnson, 44.
57 David Ansen, "We Shall Overcome," *Newsweek*, December 30, 1985, 60.
59 Leslie Rubenstein, "Oprah! Thriving on Faith," *McCall's*, December 1987, 140.
60 "Girlfriends Are Forever," *Good Housekeeping*, May 2000, 110.
61 "Oprah Winfrey: Entertainment Executive."
62 *Oprah Winfrey: Heart of the Matter*.
62–63 Ibid.

67 Laura B. Randolph, "Oprah Opens Up about Her Weight, Her Wedding and Why She Withheld the Book," *Ebony*, October 1993, 130.
69–70 Ibid.
70 Pearl Cleage, "Walking in the Light," *Essence*, June 1991, 48.
71 "Oprah Winfrey: Entertainment Executive."
72–73 Ibid.
73 "Oprah Winfrey: Entertainment Executive."
74 Joanna Powell, "I Was Trying to Fill Something Deeper," *Good Housekeeping*, October 1996, 80.
74 Ibid.
78 Lisa Russell and Cindy Dampier, "Oprah Winfrey," *People Weekly*, March 15, 1999, 143.
78 "Oprah Winfrey: Entertainment Executive."
79 Johnson, 44.
80 Ibid.
81 Arthur Bridgeforth Jr., "Internet, *Oprah*, Enliven Sluggish Book Industry," *Crain's Detroit Business*, January 18, 1999, 27.
81 Johnson, 44.
82–83 Powell, 80.

83 Ibid.

86 "Oprah Winfrey Gives Her Weight Loss Tips in New Video, 'Oprah: Make the Connection,'" *Jet*, October 20, 1997, 23.

87 Johnson, 44.

87 Ibid.

88 Laurel Brubaker Colkins and Craig Tomashoff, "Oprah 1, Beef 0," *People Weekly*, March 16, 1998, 59.

88–89 "Oprah: 'Free Speech Rocks,'" *CNN*, February 26, 1998, <http://www.cnn.com/us/9802/26/oprah.verdict/> (May 13, 2004).

91 Laura B. Randolph, "Oprah and Danny," *Ebony*, November 1998, 36.

91 Stodghill, 80.

91 Randolph, 36.

92 Johnson, 44.

92 Leslie Marshall and Dana Fineman, "The Intentional Oprah," *InStyle*, November 1998, 338.

95 "Stedman Graham," *The Seattle Times Co.*, 1997, <http://www.speakers.com/sgraham.html> (August 14, 2000).

96 "Oprah Winfrey and Beau Stedman Graham to Teach Class at Northwestern University," *Jet*, June 7, 1999, 20.

96 Lynette Clemetson, "The Birth of a Network," *Newsweek*, November 15, 1999, 60.

97 Ibid.

97–98 Allen, 67.

98 Oprah Winfrey, *O: The Oprah Magazine*, September, 2000, n.p.

98 Mimi Avins, "Flocking to the Church of Oprah," *Los Angeles Times*, June 25, 2000. Access through EBSCOhost®, EBSCO Information Services Group, article no. 000059965445082000.

98–99 Ibid.

99 Allen, 67.

100 Avins.

100–101 Powell, 112.

101 "Oprah's Birthday Weekend," *ET Online*, February 1, 2004, <http://et.tv.yahoo.com/tv/2004/02/01/oprahbirthday/> (March 15, 2004).

Selected Bibliography

Allen, Jenny. "Oprah Winfrey." *US Weekly,* June 12, 2000.

Clemetson, Lynette. "The Birth of a Network." *Newsweek,* November 15, 1999.

Culhane, John. "Oprah Winfrey: How Truth Changed Her Life." *Reader's Digest,* February 1989.

Farley, Christopher John. "Queen of All Media." *Time,* October 5, 1998.

"Girlfriends Are Forever." *Good Housekeeping,* May 2000.

Greene, Bob, and Oprah Winfrey. *Make the Connection: Ten Steps to a Better Body–and a Better Life.* New York: Hyperion, 1999.

Grossberger, Lewis. "The Story of O." *MediaWeek,* April 24, 2000.

Johnson, Marilyn. "Oprah Winfrey." *Life,* September 1997.

King, Norman. *Everybody Loves Oprah.* New York: William Morrow and Co., 1987.

Malcolm, Shawna. "Oprah Mania." *Entertainment Weekly,* September 4, 1998.

"Oprah Winfrey." *Biography,* December 1998.

Oprah Winfrey: Heart of the Matter. Produced by Eileen Lucas. 120 min. ABC Inc. and A&E Networks, 1999. Videocassette.

Powell, Joanna. "Oprah's Awakening." *Good Housekeeping,* December 1998.

Randolph, Laura B. "Oprah Opens Up About Her Weight, Her Wedding and Why She Withheld the Book." *Ebony,* October 1993.

Russell, Lisa, and Cindy Dampier. "Oprah Winfrey." *People Weekly*, March 15, 1999.

Winfrey, Oprah, and Pearl Cleage. "The Courage to Dream!" *Essence*, December 1998.

FURTHER READING AND WEBSITES

Black History Month
<http://www.galegroup.com/free_resources/bhm/>
Read biographies of African Americans, including Oprah Winfrey, who have made a difference. You can also trace events that helped shape African American heritage and explore African American literature.

Blashfield, Jean F. *Oprah Winfrey*. New York: World Almanac, 2003.

Fact Sheet: Oprah Winfrey
<http://www.eonline.com/Facts/People/Bio/0,128,16930,00 .html>
This website includes facts about Oprah Winfrey's life and a list of awards.

Kite, L. Patricia. *Maya Angelou*. Minneapolis: Lerner Publications Company, 1998.

Lazo, Caroline. *Alice Walker: Freedom Writer*. Minneapolis: Lerner Publications Company, 2000.

National Women's Hall of Fame
<http://www.greatwomen.org/>
Biographies of famous women, including Oprah Winfrey, are featured on this website, along with a list of books about them.

Oprah.com
<http://www.oprah.com/>
Oprah Winfrey's home page includes links to her magazine, *O: The Oprah Magazine*; her TV show; a biography; book club; and more.

Oprah Winfrey
<http://www.imdb.com/name/nm0001856/>
Oprah Winfrey's film credits as a producer and actress, her other performances, and guest appearances are listed in this linked website.

Stone, Tanya Lee. *Oprah Winfrey: Success with an Open Heart.* Brookfield, CT: Millbrook Press, 2001.

INDEX

PHOTO ACKNOWLEDGMENTS

Photographs are used with the permission of: © Buddy Mays/Travel Stock, p. 4; Library of Congress (LC-USZ62-125806), p. 7; AP/Wide World Photos, pp. 14, 67, 68, 89, 90, 93, 101; © John Angelos, Books, p. 18; © Bettmann/CORBIS, pp. 20, 27, 36; Classmates.com Yearbook Archives, pp. 25, 31, 38; Hollywood Book & Poster, pp. 42, 51, 52, 58, 62; © Howard Ande, p. 53; Lettuce Entertain You Enterprises, Inc., p. 65; © Jorie Gracie/London Features International (USA) Ltd., p. 66; © Joseph Marzullo/Retna Ltd., pp. 74, 75; © Maria Mulas, p. 81; © Walter McBride/Retna Ltd., p. 82; © Walter Weissman/Globe Photos, Inc., p. 84; © Mitchell Gerber/CORBIS, pp. 86, 95; Independent Picture Service, p. 97.

Cover: © Glenn Weiner/ZUMA Press.